WORDS NEVER Spoken

—A Poetry Journal for Healing

CHERYL DENISE BANNERMAN

© *2021 Cheryl Denise Bannerman. All rights reserved.*

2nd edition

No part of this book may be reproduced, stored in a retrieval system, or transmitted by any means without the written permission of the author.

ISBN: 978-0578326955 (sc)

This is a work of fiction. All of the characters, names, incidents, organizations, and dialogue in this novel are either the products of the author's imagination or are used fictitiously.

"Stand up straight and realize you are a Child of God, and with him you can tower over your circumstances." ~ Dr. Maya Angelou

This book is dedicated to my daughter:
the bravest, strongest, smartest person I know.

Table of Contents

Chapter 1   When I Was Me (back when I knew myself) 1
Reflections: Knowing Yourself 13

Chapter 2   Mr. Wonderful...15
Reflections: Your Knight..26

Chapter 3   The Two-Faces of Evil..27
Reflections: A Moment in Time..38

Chapter 4   Living in Silence 39
Reflections: Making Your Voice Heard...56

Chapter 5   The Great Escape 57
Reflections: Houdini in the Making...63

Chapter 6   Unrecognizable 65
Reflections: Who Am I?..76

Chapter 7:   Waiting for Mr. Wrong..77
Reflections: Loving Yourself...85
Reflections: Playing the Single Game..85
Reflections: Defining Your Happily Ever After..85

About the Author 89

Chapter 1

WHEN I WAS ME
(BACK WHEN I KNEW MYSELF)

I wanted what every girl wants: to fall in love and live happily ever after. But after one failed marriage and with forty quickly approaching, I had given up. Pouring my time into my child, my God, and my business was my life. So here is my story...

I Am Empowered

I am empowered
I am His Daughter
HE has my back

I am empowered
My child is His grandchild
HE has our back

I am empowered
Oh how we prosper
For nothing we lack

We are empowered
We be writin' dem checks
Wit lots of zeroes

We are His children
We are the ones you mock
We are the ones you hate

We are successful
Checks in the mail
Everyone knows our name

We are His children
Unique in our own way
Never the same

I am empowered by her
She is empowered by me
We are as One

I am empowered by her
She is empowered by me
We are His Children

Try as you may
Try as you will
Won't take that pill

Blue or Red, I ain't dead
Eternal Life

Neva givin' up
That's what's up
Through pain and strife

I am empowered
I am empowered
This is my life

I am empowered
Let me empower you
I live for HIS glory

I am empowered
I AM empowered
I AM EMPOWERED

This was who I was.

Oh, You Tryin' Me, huh?

Picture it. 2001. Cranbury, New Jersey.
A scared little girl clinging to her mama's leg.
Lookin' up like 'she don't know that man'.

I thought I knew that man.
Had a baby with that man.
Married that man.
Divorced that man.
But I ain't know that man.

A scared little girl clinging to her mama's leg.

Classified as separation anxiety, ADHD, and blah blah blah
Somethin' ain't right
Is you tryin' me, Satan?

A scared little girl hiding in small spaces
Hot with the fire of anger
Confused and alone

A mama scared to face the truth
The results are in
Yep. He tryin' me. The **ULTIMATE** test.

As the envelope and letter fell to the floor
My body followed
My legs nor my God could hold me up

A scared little girl clinging to her mama's leg

Doctors. Disclosures. Court dates.
Went on for years.
A scared little girl with endless tears.

Two years and counting
More litigation
White man in a robe sayin' he deserve visitation

You don't know me
Or my scared little girl
Scars that will NEVA heal

Innocence snatched away
Like a wig in a cat fight
You don't know me Mr. white man in a robe

Oh, yes, he tryin' me.
Watchin' CSI mocking up my plan
Wonderin' if anyone 'knew of' a man

Can anyone help me?
Can he just roam free?
For what he did to my baby and me

A scared little girl clinging to her mama's leg.

Picture it. 2003. South Orange, New Jersey.
The verdict is in
A scared little girl dries her tears. The Healing begins.
She don't know that man

Growin' up STILL that scared little girl…clinging to her mama's leg.
Clinging to Her Father
Hanging on to Faith
Praying for peace
I told you Satan NOT to try me…cause we know THAT Man.

Becoming a Nun

I only got two damn hands
And it's only but so many more 'fantasies' in my head

Girlfriends are trying
Or tryin' to get in my bed

Dating sites are for losers
Who just want sum head

Can a sista get a life?

The Internet. Ha!
Why can't you be who you say you are?
Live close to me and not so far.
Not have 10 kids and baby drama.
Have a job and not live wit yo mama.
Is that too much to ask?

Gettin' used to goin' this life alone
All dressed up with nowhere to go
Waitin' for that knight in shinin' armor
But, wait, I don't do no damn horses, so nevamind

Anyway, as I was saying, A-L-O-N-E
Pathetic is ME
Watching Mad TV on a Saturday night
Outside my window; world's passin' me by
Don't care for the drink or the smoke
Don't do weed, meth or coke
So that makes me B-O-R-I-N-G in 2010
Damn, where are the MEN!
Am I askin' too much?

I only got two damn hands
And it's only but so many more 'fantasies' in my head

Tossin' and turnin'
Watching the sun fall
Thinkin' of which Ex I could call
I need it bad

Got an offer to speed date
But that's way too fast
Got a call from a matchmaker
But ain't got the cash

Been to the library, church and the market
And found me a sugah daddy
Get me twenty dollars here and there (big up to Mike Epps)

Seriously though, at the end of the day
My needs unmet
Panties wet
...patience is a virtue that I DON'T have
I only got two damn hands
And ima use 'em tonight!

Bye Felicia!

Reflections: Knowing Yourself

Name all the things you LOVE about yourself when you are single.

_____
_____
_____
_____
_____
_____

Name all the things you LOVE about yourself when you are coupled.

_____
_____
_____
_____
_____
_____

Compare (1) and (2). Are they the same or different? In a good or bad way?

_____
_____
_____
_____
_____
_____
_____

Chapter 2

MR. WONDERFUL

Well, that day has finally come for me. I hit the jackpot ladies and the winnings are all mine. Here's how it went down...

Stella

Got my groove back bitches
Bye Grim Reaper
Met 'em on the Internet, and this one's a keeper

Nigga got a job, a car, and a … well, you know
With a smile that charms and an appetite for… you know
I ain't lonely no mo'!

Divorced like me wit one kid, jus' like me
Been down and out, jus' like me
Lookin' for love, jus' like me
He whispers in my ear, 'lets make this official'
I said, "You had me at Let's".

Fun days and endless nights
You could tell by my walk, I ain't put up a fight
But I ain't one to kiss and tell

Soon my abode became his own
Along with all his shit
And I officially buckled in for the ride, bitches

You can't tell me nothin'
Got me sum eye candy on my arm
With his sexy swag and New York charm

Ain't sayin' he's perfect
Got a few bad habits
But I'm blinded by the D

Been over a year
I was turned UP and OUT
You couldn't tell me nuthin'

Friends and family in my biz
Givin' their two cents
But I can't hear you tho

Just call me Stella
I ain't neva skurred
So you best beware
Telling anyone who asks who he belong to

Or so I thought?

Nigga Seddy

Nigga seddy he had a job, *just started*
Nigga seddy he had one kid, *had five*
Nigga seddy he had a house, *had a room*
Nigga seddy he was smoked on occasion, *was a weed head*

I should walk away RIGHT NOW
But I don't

Thinkin of that 'one thing' like Amerie said
'member, I ain't neva skurred

I can be a ride or die chic
I can be cool
Betta than being alone again

Six months later I'm already feeling you
More shit comes into view
I cover my ears and start singing. I can't listen.

Here we go…

Nigga seddy he had a past, *understatement of the year*
Nigga seddy he served time, *drug possessions with an s*
Nigga seddy he had a job, *been lying leaving for work every morning*
Nigga seddy he was like no other, *damn sure right*

I should walk away RIGHT NOW
But I don't

This ain't the way I was raised
This ain't the knight I was waiting for
Who in the hell left the gate open?

But God said not to judge
Help people in need
You have officially become my Project

Ima help you see the light [congregation in background: Yesss!]
Walk you to the altar [congregation in background: Thank you Jesus!]
Remove the seddy from your life [congregation in background: Praise Him!]
Can I get an AMEN church?! [congregation in background: Hallelujer! – in the words of Madea]

So there you have it, the cat is officially out of the bag
I was in love with the IDEA of being in love
In love with the man I knew he COULD be
Ain't that a bitch.

I should walk away RIGHT NOW
But I won't

Supaman

Look up in the sky, it's a bird, it's a plane
Nope, it's just my man
And he's still fuckin' lame

Leaping from job to job in a single bound
Tall enough to fuck four bitches at one time, and not get caught
Or so he thought?
[Homey don't play dat]

With him I felt safe and secure
As long as Henney wasn't around
He ALWAYS stole the show when he was around

I felt like the hottest woman in the room when we were out
Unless a fat ass walked by
Then I became the 2nd hottest woman in the room

But I love the way he makes me feel
The way he looks at me, deep into my eyes
And then breathes smoke in my face

I love his juicy lips and the way he kisses me
When he says he'll be right back
And shows up the next morning

I love the way he cherishes our special moments
Remembering places we visited together
*Until I realize **I've** never been there*

I love the way he slides up in me
And takes it nice and slow
And then passes out mid-stroke in a drunken stupor
I love this man dammit
He's mine and no one else's
He's MY supaman

Powerful enough to charm the smartest woman
Out of her house, her money, and her dignity
A woman with multiple graduate degrees and certifications
A business-savvy entrepreneur, who lacks what my daddy called 'street smarts'

But how could this be, you ask?
How could this happen?
Why is that lawyer calling him a 'slippery snake'?
What does everyone else see that I don't?
How much more of this could I take?

What kind of 'tom foolery' is this?
Why can't you see what I see?

Can't you see him? He is supaman!
See him flying through the skies?
See him leap tall buildings?
Watch him charm his way into any job?
He can do ANYTHING

What kind of 'tom foolery' is this?
Why can't you see what I see?

Why are they pointing and staring at me?
I'm with supaman dammit!
Don't tell me what you know about him, you know NOTHING!
Only I know supaman's secrets.

What his mama did to him?
What the streets did to him?
The pain in his throat when he chokes through the tears

Telling his story with the help of Henney
For the umpteenth time
But still painful to hear

Only I know supaman's secrets.
Stories of incest, abuse and drugs.
A young boy forced to become a man on the streets of New York
Only I know.

My supaman can overcome!
You don't know him like I do.
And you never will.
Only I can help him.
I CAN help him.

I CAN HELP him.

As I lower my head, he lifts my chin
And slowly brushes my lips with his
"I am anything you want me to be
And <u>only</u> yours FOREVER."

And then I awoke

Reflections: Your Knight

What did your Knight in Shining Armor or Princess/Queen look like as a child?

_____
_____
_____
_____
_____
_____
_____
_____
_____

What does your Knight in Shining Armor or Princess/Queen look like (through your eyes) today?

_____
_____
_____
_____
_____
_____
_____
_____
_____

Chapter 3

THE TWO-FACES OF EVIL

I've seen mood swings before, I've seen drug addictions, I've seen alcoholics. Hell, my father was one. But I never been in a relationship with someone who had ALL OF THE ABOVE. Girl, let me school you...

Drunk in Love

I obviously had Beyonce's song all wrong
I'm up here drunk in love and this nigga's just drunk

We goin' from high to low
Happy to Sad
Giddy to Depressed
Hyper to Sleepy
And Drunk to High
In one goddamn day. What the hell?

I'm livin' with Pookie from New Jack City
And I don't know if I'm comin' or goin'
If you don't get the hell out of my house

3 am calls from the police
'Come git your nigga, he seddy liv wit' you'
Ain't this a bitch

Now I got two kids I gotta raise, and I only carried <u>one</u> for nine months
So why do I feel like I'm in labor again?
Crawled up in the corner of the bed, in the fetal position, crying

Did I hear somewhere that love wasn't supposed to hurt?
Boy did they git that fucked up
This shit hurt like hell

Bruises on my arms and legs
Hand marks around my neck
Jabs to my self-esteem
Words that cut like a machete
And then after, make-up sex marking 3.0 on the Richter scale

All was fine in my world again until the calls began
Phone blowing up
Stepping out to talk
Girl interrupted

Ex is in the picture
All up in the frame
How much more could I take?

My tolerance must be either high or non-existent
Six years go by and I'm hanging on for dear life
I ain't neva skurred

Until now…

Henney

I was one of the bears that just came home
"Someone's been sleeping in my bed" I said
A bottle of Henney sittin' on the nightstand

Cheatin' on me with that bitch again
With her buttery brown skin and lips that tempt the soul
Voulez vous coucher avec moi?, she whispers

With promises to make him forget
She was the blues in his left thigh... trying to become the funk in his right.
That ain't alright with me, NO.

It was my job to make him forget
My job to heal all his wounds
But I ain't as smooth as her goin' down

He often took her to the head, licking his lips in delight
As she cried and begged for more
That whore.

What does she have that I don't?!
She ain't got breasts like me, with hips that sway
Intoxicating eyes and a killer smile. I'm just sayin'.

What does she have that I don't?!

The promise to take him higher
Higher than he's eva been before
Higher than the clouds; looking down at his problems below, jus laughin'

What is so damn funny?!
And why won't you eat?
Don't touch me. I hate you.
Dangerous words that mean 'I can't breathe without you' from a sista
I'm just sayin'.

Her seductive ways take him higher,
Making him happy, sad, and paranoid all in one breath
I can't go on, he cries…taking her to his mouth again.
She moans in pleasure.
Best head she eva got.
I'm just sayin'.

Soon she will steal him away for good
She's already in my bed, my house, my home
She's seduced him with her smooth silky taste that burns so good

She's already stolen his dignity, his drive, his manhood
Life fallin' to pieces like Dominoes
He has no idea how to get up out da bed

The more doors that close
The more No's in his ear
The more he turns to her
That bitch.

Promising to solve all his problems one at a time.
Graduating from a pint to a fifth, almost overnight.
This bitch has moved herself into my home. Damn.

Wait, wait, no, you can't invite her other friend!
A mena jay twah in my home! In my bed!
Who does this bitch think she is?

He scrambles and searches for his 'special' light
The one with the Libra that I bought him one night
Her friend is ready to try sum of the best head she'll eva have.

He brings her to his mouth and sucks hungrily.
She moans in return.
He chokes for a second, and lets the exhale begin.
A slow burn that feels almost as good as Henney.
I'm so done.

Soon he is doing both of them at the same time.
Right in front of me.
Making him happy, sad, and paranoid all in one breath.
Except now, the bedroom stinks of his 'lovemaking'.

Days, weeks, months, years go by, wit' me as the 'otha woman'.
The mena jay twah continues. I took a back seat to the hoes.
I can't compete with this shit.
He still has no idea how to get up out da bed

The more doors that close.
The more No's in his ear.
The more he turns to them.
The song was right…Bitches ain't shit but hoes and tricks.
As I listen to sobbing in the background over an ole Kelly Price track.

From zero to a hunned too quick
What once was sadness and despair turned into hunger and laughter
An hour later, the source of all his problems was solved. It was me.

Turns out I was the cause of the mena jay twah,
The doors that closed, the No's in his ear,
and everything else that went wrong in his life.
The mystery had been solved. I wasn't 'holding him down' in the way that I thought. Ha!

As the anger builds, the two hoes stay in his ear
Talkin' about me like I ain't even there
He vows to make me pay.
This time… I'm skurred.

One Eye Open

Oh where oh where has my gentle man went?
Oh where oh where can he be?
I thought, as I lay on 'my side of the bed' once again.
Eyes burning from sleepin' with one eye open.

Up all night, and not from good lovin'
It was the weekend, and mena ja toi's turn for that.
While I hide in my office prayin' for a good night's sleep.
I lost count after the 100th sheep.

Wipin' the sleep out my eyes I proceed to nudge him awake for his 3rd job this month
I buckle up and brace for impact, 5 – 4 – 3 – 2 – 1
A lovin' husband grabs me and snuggles my neck. Whew!
The day ahead is good. Or so I thought.

Shirts pressed, lunch packed and out the door!
I'm home free and my man is off to work!
Now to catch up on some Z's and get my sexy back.
Or so I thought.

Two hours into a wet dream with Morris Chestnut, my one eye opened.
Keys jingling the lock, stumbled footsteps, the sound of hoes giggling.
You have got to be kiddin' me.

Footsteps stompin' up the steps, I closed my one eye and faked sleep
Minutes later the 'crew' was in bed with me and all hope was lost.
"It's just not a good fit." he was told. Checks in the mail.
Unable to stand the stench, my wet dream was officially over.
Sorry Morris. Next time.

It was groundhog day.

Wipin' the sleep out my eyes I proceed to nudge him awake for his 3rd job this month
I buckle up and brace for impact, 5 – 4 – 3 – 2 –

Not making it to one. The sting on my arm was overwhelming as I wrestled with sheets.
Struggling to become 'untangled' in a morning two-step that had no rhythm.
I was a terrible dancer.

I was 'every name in the book', 'not like the others', and 'making him sick'.
Not 'feminine' or 'sweet' or able to suck, well you know.
The barrage of threats continued as the booming voice pierced my very soul.
Every word tattooed on my brain. I was no longer whole.

Escaping the two-step I scrambled down the steps for cover.
Nothing coffee and a good meal can't fix!
I said to myself as I rubbed the purple outline beginning to form on my bicep.
Nothing coffee and a good meal can't fix!

Calm, smooth and debonair used his swag to descend the staircase.
Smelling good and ready to seize the day.
Singing a Carl Thomas tune I've heard many times before.
The morning two-step was already forgotten.

As he grabbed and kissed me, I winced in pain.
He inquired about my arm.
"Must've slept on it the wrong way" I lied.
The morning two-step had already been forgotten.

It was groundhog day.
I thought, as I lay on 'my side of the bed' once again.
Eyes burnin' from sleeping with one eye open.
The alarm chirps. Well, here we go again. 5 – 4 – 3 –

Reflections: A Moment in Time

If you could take back any moment in time, what would it be and why?

_____
_____
_____
_____
_____
_____
_____
_____
_____

If you could tell someone from your past how they helped you become the person you are today, who would it be and what would you say to them?

_____
_____
_____
_____
_____
_____
_____
_____
_____

Chapter 4

LIVING IN SILENCE

How's that old song go? Break up to make up. Hmph! More like 'He loves me, he loves me not, he hurts me, he's sorry again'. Ha! And I, like a fool, believe AND forgive him.

Reminds me of the symbol for infinity, around and around in a circle of pain and pleasure. The ultimate addiction. I can't get enough of him, yet I've had enough of him. My voice has been silenced…temporarily.

The Faceless Man

All I feel is your muscle deep inside me as I wrap my legs around your slim frame
Unspeakable words escape my lips, as the tension from the week slips away
I belong to you

As the pace quickens I opened my eyes to drink in the sexiness like a cool drink of water
But the gasp escaped my lips before I could stop it
He was back

The faceless man with the black hole set upon his neck was starin' into my soul
Was I looking at my own reflection, or was it real?
The fear encases me

Fear mixed with pleasure as we thrust our hips towards climax as one
Me wanting to exit this place as soon as he, well you know
So I faked it

Standing under the cascades of hot water I drown in despair
Rinsing the filth from my lady parts
I remember the black hole

Was he always faceless, or had I always been a blank
Did I ever have my own identity, I cannot recall
The memories are now a black hole

A prized possession for his pleasures, to do with as he chose
Any time of the day or night, his wish was my command
It was me who had no face

Running to the mirror, wiping away the steam
I struggle to see a face
But there is nothing there
I am faceless

Stripped to the core
Stripped of dignity
So desperate for a man
I am empty.

It is I who is faceless.

I am the con artist, NOT HIM
He was always this way, and I was always this blind
Now I am faceless

Nowhere to run or hide.
No one will ever want you.
He laughs to my face. I can no longer see.

Confused and alone, Scared and alone, Sad and alone.
I am surrounded by people, women, breasts, asses...
Where am I?

Hands groping me. Tearing at my clothes.
What is this place? Where am I?
Was I always this way?
His wish was my command.

Trying to say no, but the Novocain has me numb
He only wants to, well you know
Too bad if you don't get yours, he laughs
His wish was my command.

Again he is on top, and I shut my eyes real tight
Hold on with all my might
Waiting for the ride to end, to wash away this filth
I was never this way

I was never this way

I was never this way

What room are we in now? Was it always this small?
Pass me an inhaler, would you please?
I can't breathe

Another night gown torn
Another mark, another scar
When will it be too far?

On my knees like a dog, staring at a spot on the wall
Waiting for the ride to end, and him to fall off
His slumber awaits

Once and for all I will reveal his face
Lift the mask and solve this enigma
The time has come

You are the faceless man, I am for real!
As I scream in my head, make the big reveal

No! It can't be! I was never this way
He was always this way, and I was always this blind

Now I am faceless.

The Bathroom Floor

The S on my chest was itching more than usual on this day
Another 'side chic' has surfaced
I am not a Superwoman, but a Scarlet

A Scarlet branded with a hot iron of fire
Verbal lashes of the whip leave imprints on my back
No salve could heal my wounds

I was mentally trained for this challenge
From a girl of youth to adulthood
It was my destiny

A kindness smelt from a mile away
I was easy prey
A good girl some would say

Yes, the S on my chest was itching more than usual on this day
As I shudder from the cold tile
The razor beside me

The town tried to warn me, it fell on deaf ears
I was mesmerized by his charm
And what lies beneath it

Now it was me who was cold
Shivering from the ice in his eyes
The callous of his remarks

Tossed aside as a baby, failing in health
Overweight and without enough wealth
Oh the callous of his remarks

Beat down to the tile of my favorite room
I was there to end it all on this day…again
The razor still beside me

If only I hadn't said this or that
If only you weren't so this and that
I would have never strayed…again

The razor laid beside me

Contemplating who will care for my child
The burning S glowed like a fire gone wild
She was the air I breathe

Hearing her laugh as the line was drawn
The edge sunk deep
The blood flowed strong
Onto the cold, cold tile

The stained razor laid beside me
As I drifted off in peace
Ahhhhh, no more pain

A loud crash, a scream, my body lifted
Warm water drowning my spirit
My knight had arrived

Words were taken back but the S still burned
Unable to wash away
A woman branded for life
With an S on her chest

A knight holding his queen under the stream of water
For a moment in time, I thought he was mine
Our tears intertwined

Bandaged and clean, the sleep taken over
I was loved once again
Until another 'side chic' surfaced

The cold tile callin' my name

Losing Myself

Was raised in the church, always knew right from wrong
White gloved women shushing me and my cousins to silence
As fast-flicking wrists waved paper fans every which way but up

Respect your elders, say yes ma'am and thank you
Hold the door open for ladies
And add a Miss to everyone your mama called by first name; she ain't yo friend, she mine

Sneaking a candy before dinner
Saying you didn't have no homework when you did
Was the furthest I'd ever gone on the White Lie spectrum; a soft shade of yellow I'd guess

Then Mr. Wonderful comes along with a new rule book
Some new plays I ain't neva seen before
Says I could make it to the playoffs if I just try a few. Hmmph.

I'm waking in a cold sweat. Game day was here
Coach was ready to put me in position before all the other hoes
I'm just standing there dumbfounded as that damn white-gloved usher gives me the stink eye

I could feel a bead of sweat trickle down the back of my neck
My mother and father were in the stands waiting for my decision
Would I play by his rules or use my old playbook? The one I was raised on.

Scriptures of sin, forgiveness and hell floated around my head
I was remembering Catechisms from third grade, aw man.
Coach wants an answer now and he ain't playin' neither. It's either you or the hoes.

Silence filled the stadium as I muttered the two words Coach was not expecting to hear
I Can't.
The crowd went wild as I held my head high for his reply.

He knew I wasn't built for these plays, being replaced by the hoes
Go sit the bench and I'll call you when I need you
It was the ultimate betrayal, but my proudest day yet

Ain't nobody ever stood up to Coach like that before, I was the first
Took his plays like the requirements for a new job
Do as you're told and don't ask questions…or else.

My mama and daddy didn't raise no fool
I may be naïve but my faith runs deep
Won't be puttin' my name on no dotted line, for the devil in disguise

Won't be forgin' no papers or lyin' through my teeth
So the white man can put me in his jail
That's like makin' a decision between heaven and hell

So I took the Coach's abuse and sat the bench.
Watched the hoes, smelled the stench.
And waited til' it was my turn again.

Satan had failed again, thinkin' I'd be hungry for that fruit
But I turn't the tables on that red snake once again
I ain't neva losing myself, or my faith, for anyone.
Not even for
Mr. Wonderful.

Fighting Back

It was days before the deed
Episodes of CSI run through my head
I was becoming the two faces of evil. Damn.

The empty barrel looked like a dark, one-way tunnel
And I was neva coming back
Looking down at the pile of silent killers in front of me

You can find anything on the Internet
How to kill yourself, how to kill others, how to molest a child
I was holding back the bile in my throat as I read each line

Silent killers, plant killers, pill killers
Bullet killers, knife killers…hell, even hiring killers!
I had had enough

Holding my ribs from last night's 'dance'
I had fought back too hard
Bitch had to learn a lesson, you know

So here I sit embracing the cold steel
Making love to its smooth skin and its power to kill
I had definitely had enough

Don't wanna wake my baby though
So I rummaged through the pile
Finding just the right one for me to garnish Sunday dinner wit
You don't care about me, you don't love me or my child
I choked through my tears
This was gonna be a tough call

He loves me, he loves me not
Damn if I know
I done went from wife to just a side ho

Bitches callin' my phone now, laughin' at me
Mind games played to the umpteenth degree
I had more than enough

I wanna look in his eyes when he feels what I've felt
Ten years of cheating, abuse, and more
As the lights go out, I'll be your whore.

Oh shit! He's comin' for me! Hide the stash!
The oo-wee got him ragin' and he itchin' for a fight
We struggle.

For.

The.

Gun.

BANG! BANG! BANG! My new sheets were ruined.
My mouth froze in horror like a case of lock jaw.
My vocal chords awaken and I …
Scream.

Bloody.

Murder.

My throat is so sore.
My eyes see nothing but RED.
I can't stop shaking.

Back and forth, Back and forth. I can't stop shaking.
Childlike whispers in my ear
Mommy, mommy, are you okay?

No longer seeing RED, but rays of sunlight
It was the break of dawn
My ray of sunshine had saved me again.

Today is another day the Lord has made.
I WILL survive.

Lonely Together

Sitting in church with baby girl
Waitin' for you to walk in with your fine self
I knew better than to hold my breath
The end is near

Sleeping back to back
Front to Front
Don't really matter, I was still a cunt…to him, anyway
The end is near

I had many names, baby girl did too
Won't repeat them for you
Ain't trying to give ammo to the next guy
The end is here

Going over a friend's house
Don't wait up
A phrase gone on deaf ears
As I sit by the window

Text message at two am
You made me do it,
You pushed me away
Too high to drive home
I'm still sittin' by the window

Leavin' work as I pick up baby girl
She was no longer his care
He says with a smirk
Oh, he tryin' me fer real.

Washing his hands of it all
He makes a call. I listen to his swag.
Another new chic.
On the phone that I pay for, ain't that a bitch.
The end is.

Told that judge we meant forever
Through the good and bad
Now we lonely together

No money for counselin', got his bills to pay
I'm holdin' him down while he finds his way
Holdin' him down, while his thang stay up
Just not for me
In a way I was free

So we lonely together
I can just be alone
Do bad by myself, there was no one else
Jus' me and baby girl
She was my whole world

So, I vowed to be lonely
Vowed to stay alone
I'm SO gone.

The end.

Reflections: Making Your Voice Heard

Is your voice heard in relationships? If not, how can you make it heard in a positive way?

_____
_____
_____
_____
_____
_____
_____
_____

Do you or someone you know suffer from depression or attempted to commit suicide? How does that experience change a person's life? Or maybe it affected your life? Do you now see life differently?

_____
_____
_____
_____
_____
_____
_____
_____

Chapter 5

THE GREAT ESCAPE

Girl, I was lost and could not be found. I had lost my faith, my identity, my dignity, my savings, and much more. And I don't even know how I got to this place. My daughter was a witness to way too much of this nonsense and it was time to go. Disrespecting me in my own home, the one that I pay all the bills for, that was the last straw. Lord give me strength…here it goes ya'll.

He Loves Me

He loves me, he loves me not
The answer lies in the petals on the floor
Should I stay or should I go?

I contemplate my life as I stare at the white cement walls
The smell of antiseptic in the air
And screams heard in the distance…down the hall

Feeling homesick and safe at the same time
I remember fragments of the crash
Loneliness, despair, and the inability to find my way home

Calling on my two Fathers in heaven
Wondering what HE thought of my current state
Did I still make Him proud?

As the visit draws near I savor every mouthful of jello
Thinking how good it taste to eat in peace
Wondering if I should make a will before exiting the building

He was coming
Not He up there, but he, the man who calls himself my husband
It was time for discharge from the safe haven

Minor injuries and a prescription to return to the safe place in my mind, at any time
He grabbed my bags and squeezed tight
Oh the irony of it all. No one is proud of me now.

Pulling the covers over my tear-stained face, I sink into the mattress
Wishing it would suck me in forever
He has entered the room

Smelling of cheap perfume and sexting messages to the unknown
I can smell the betrayal a mile away
My absence was a celebration of freedom.

Cheryl Denise Bannerman

And back to life I came.
Now sinking my face into my baby girl's neck
I hugged her tight as she slept in peace.

With a notebook in hand, I documented the cons before pros
Should I stay or should I go?
He swears promises of sweet kisses and how he loves me so

Promises on top of promises, you are the only one for me
A layer cake of delicious affairs he cannot resist
A world wide web of delights I could never be

No way to compete, so much defeat
Holding my head in pain, as it continued to beat
Father would want more for his grandchild to be
A year of planning, will it come to fruition
Ain't no light at the end of this tunnel
I can barely see from the glare of re-condition

Brainwashed as it may be, I can't see the truth
I am ugly, I am fat, and I am of no use
To anyone, to no one, your child or a man, he laughs
Now I know I must go.

He forces a makeup, "assume the position"
My mind wanders off to my own rendition
The deed is done, and the fire is out

The smell of rose petals
The splash of hot water
I am cleansed and made new from His love

Now I know I must go.

I Dare You

Thought the grass was greener on the other side, did you?
I am a scorned woman with power and money
You can't steal my joy

Beaten down 'til I lost all faith, in who I was
Beaten down just becuz…
I was there

You won't have to look at me any more
Go be with your whores
I'm a woman of God, His daughter

Go ahead and leave the house for the day
Tempt me as you may
I dare you

With the click of the lock
I dial the number for Peace
They were five minutes away

Back-breaking work, but worth the pain
Was I suffering in vain?
Only time will tell

Second thoughts clouding my joy
Stifling the efforts of many
Should I stay or should I go?
I could hear him laughing
Go ahead, you'll be back
With everything you lack

I pushed on 'til sundown
Made one last round
The deed was done

Not a chair in sight
Not even a light
The deed was done

No forwarding address
No eye witness
The deed was done

You dared me to do it
You put me through it
I could bear no more pain

Memories of our child
Nestled in my womb
As I crashed against the wall

Bounced off the bed
Gazing down at the red
I knew the deed was done

You were not the one
The one my Father spoke of
The Knight in Shining Armor

My womb was grieving
My chest heaving
With tears of remorse

You dared me
Now I know
I should go

Reflections: Houdini in the Making

Do you know someone who has a dependency with two faces of evil? How do you communicate with each side? Is it the same, or are there differences with each face?

_____
_____
_____
_____
_____
_____
_____
_____

What are some of the ways this character can re-build her life, her relationship with her child, and her self-esteem?

_____
_____
_____
_____
_____
_____
_____
_____
_____

Chapter 6

UNRECOGNIZABLE

Angry, bitter, depressed, sad, horny, happy, at peace and miserable. These were all of the emotions I was experiencing inside of me. Another failed marriage, a miscarriage, and now, both me and my daughter in therapy. Not what I envisioned my life to be at 40. But I know I can overcome with the help of both my Fathers in heaven.

Peace

Can you hear that? It's the sound of my heart beatin' fast
Don't know how long this silence will last
I was free

Can you see that? It's my laptop screen
No hidden agendas
I was finally free

Can you smell that? The smell of potpourri
No stale liquor or blunts
No urine in bottles scattered about
I was truly free

Now there was peace, so sleep came easy
I was in my own space
Free to stretch out and snore as loud as can be
I am free

Seeing the sunlight through the trees
My balcony view is a sight to see
Even the air smells fresher over here. Wow.

Work is one hunned, baby girl is thrivin'
Writin' them checks with lots of zeros
The God in me was glowing

Wear what you like, shop when you like
See your doctors in peace
It was a new day dawning for baby girl and me

Peace has been found, to God be the glory
I lived to tell yet another story
Life was worth living

For now.

Identity Crisis

Staring at the faces dressed in all black
Thinkin' they should've been red

Hugs and smiles, condolences all around
Don't call me if you need anything. I won't pick up.

Seein' my daddy's face, hearin' my mommy's laugh
A warm arm pulled me close. It wasn't them. Ugh.

White teeth through fake smiles is all I see
They all knew the truth but me

I was a bastard child. Unwanted by one.
Wanted by two. Confused by it all. The irony unspoken.

Cousins became sisters. Aunts became nannas. I became zero.
I was unwanted by one, wanted by two, and confused by it all.

Who the fuck am I? What is my name?
Was I just a pawn in this sick, twisted game?

Even the mirror lies, as I touch every feature
Remembering the similar faces I called mom and dad

The features were a match, the one was a lie
Unwanted. Hell no. A truth I deny.

Did I dream the good life? The love and the laughter.
Just like I dreamed the happily ever after.

Hell no. It was real! I was loved. I had a name.
Staring at my footprint on the green hospital form.

Lies.
Lies.
Lies.

Who am I?

Staring at photographs trying to find a match.
The marking did not align. More lies.

Do I stand my ground? Or let it go?
Can I live with the truth I may never know?

Do I go by the name on the green hospital form?
A black face, unknown, has returned. Who am I?

Once again, picking up pieces of a face off the floor
Eyes,
Noses,
Chins.
I can't find not ONE that looks like mine.

Finally, I see. They will always match the ones that wanted me
I was their child.
And the lies evaporated like water into the air.

Who am I? I may never know 'her' truth.
But truth be told, I am somebody.
I am me.
I was loved.
I am love.

Trimmin' the Hedges

Only eighty degrees outside, but one hundred in here
Cheek pressed against the cold pane lickin' my lips
Wonderin' if he could keep up with the swing of my hips. I got it bad.

Been a bit, okay a year, since I shut the door to the past.
Not sure how long this celibacy can last.
Touchin' myself, still pressed against the pain. Let the games begin.

As he lifts his shirt to wipe the sweat off his face.
I watch the beads of sweat travel downward to places unknown.
Places I wish I could explore.

As he trimmed my hedges, I was imagining the same.
Every Thursday at three, it was me who ----, well you get the point.
I'm singing 'Should I give him some? ...Maybe.' (Thanks to Toni)

In my best sundress I did my best 'sashay'
Offered him some cold water for a hot, hot day
Thanked him for doing such a good job on my bushes. Ha!

A caramel version of Denzel hungrily devoured the water
A thirst I could relate to, as he licked his lips
He was hungry for more

Sure, you can use my restroom. It's right down the hall.
His bowlegged swagger intoxicating.
I should give him some.
Said he had noticed me in the window every week.
Wondered why I was sneakin' a peak...as he trimmed the hedges
I was officially in heat

Offering more water I headed to the fridge
But was stopped in mid stride by the long arm of the 'lawn'
He was thirsty for somethin' better and I had just the thing

Kitchen counters scattered with clothing, dishes pushed aside
Lips touching lips, stride matching stride
I was holding on for dear life ya'll

It had been over a year, yet the ride was real
I was ready and he was steel
Yet I still felt like I was cheatin' on my husband

How can this be? He had hoes by the hundreds
Why can't I get a little sumthin'?
Why can't I feel again?

The strides quickened and the climax was near
What should be joy, seem to turn into fear
I was backing down from the fight, and then…

Two strong hands grabbed each side of my face
And green eyes locked with mine
I was back in the game

Two as one, we lay swathed in our sex
Smiles of exhaustion covered our faces
Whispers in my ear, words of praises…and what not

My leg was still shakin' when the doorbell rang
The mirror said I looked fine, but the butterflies spoke otherwise
It was caramel Denzel with my invoice for the week

As he thanked me for the water I watched him walk away
Wondering if I had time for just one more fantasy…
Nahhhh. Let it be. 'See you next Thursday at three.'

Life

Church
Prayer
The Word
Strength
I was holdin' on

Therapy
Pills
Sharp objects
Bloody floors
She was holdin' on

Drive-bys
Phone calls
Emails
Texts
He was holdin' on

Pain
Repeat
Pain
Betrayal
I was letting go

Love
Life
Laughter
A new home
She was coming back

Wounds
Healing
Pain
Bonding
We were moving on

Drive-bys
Phone calls
Emails
Texts
He was still holdin' on

Threats
Tantrums
Break-ins
Phone calls
The grip was stifling

Knocking
Alarms
Fear
The Chase
We were gasping for air

ENOUGH
Dis
A
Pear
We were moving on

Happiness
Smiles
Peace
Healing
We were tryin' again

Church
Prayer
The Word
Strength
Never left me.

I AM FREE.

Reflections: Who Am I?

Have you ever felt a time in your life when you have lost yourself? Lost your identity? Things you used to do, you don't do anymore? Friends become distance memories. Your interests have taken a back seat to someone or something else. You end up asking yourself, "Who am I?"

Share your thoughts below.

_____
_____
_____
_____
_____
_____
_____
_____
_____
_____
_____
_____
_____
_____
_____
_____
_____
_____
_____

Chapter 7:

WAITING FOR MR. WRONG

So, what now? Still divorced and single, working to support my child, and trying to love myself again. I know what I want and what to look for now, but I know I'm not ready to look. So, I stay single and serving God and contemplate what it is I am trying to accomplish in this life.

Incomplete

A friend of mine once told me to look in the mirror
Say 'I love you' and show forgiveness
I couldn't even look her in the eye

If only I had really listened to the peanut gallery
They had seen his kind before
They marry the good girls and sleep with the whores

Can't forgive myself for overlooking the lies
The sneakin', the cheatin', the false alibis
Promises to love me harder had turned me out. And I loved the attention

Now I was alone, trying to love myself, once again
Certain of what I like and don't like in a man
But not ready for that first step on the moon. Zero gravity.

You can run but you can't hide. My Confidence calls for me.
The body wants what the mind can't see. I don't deserve...
Damn, there I go again, blocking my friend. Him and S. Esteem

You are NOT stupid, fat, ugly or blind
The medical conditions of yours do NOT define
You ARE more than just body parts and a good time

Say it aloud until it doesn't hurt no mo'
Sitting in her special chair, glasses propped on her nose
My life neatly written in cryptic notes. That shit don't work

Tell me something I don't know
Tell me how to get his voice out my head
Tell me how to wake up from the nightmares that keep me runnin' skurred

How do I stop putting my own self down?
Beating myself down as if I were his fist
You can tell me how to do that? Well, can you?!

You can't tell me 'cause you don't know what it feels like
To watch someone you love steal away with others
Secret calls, secret chat rooms, secret profiles, secret lovers

You can't tell me what it feels to not know your worth
Tryin' to get answers from those that raised you
When they're no longer here on this forsaken earth

The healing starts from within
And you can't tell me how to do it
You can only smile and pretend you know my pain

Stumbling down the path I think He wants me to take
I submerge myself in worship and prayer
Another mistake I cannot afford to make

Took much time, too much wasted time
Yet He tells me that it is not so
I was not a pawn in some game. I was meant to learn and grow

So wiser and stronger I join Confidence on the sidelines
S. Esteem comes over and eases my mind. He's here to stay
Not sure for how long, so ima have to keep praying. I can't walk this path alone

Confidence comes and goes, he travels for work, not that stable
I join S. Esteem for lunch whenever I'm able
But the relationships die down over time

Back to worship and prayer, I stay on the path
The path of righteousness and good deeds
Tithing, honoring Him, planting the seeds. HE should be sending someone soon. Right?

More sessions on the couch, telling me how to feel
Thinking she knows what will make my mind heal
Only God knows what will heal all my wounds. Only God

So day after day, I take a step at a time
I do all the deeds, and say all the lines
But never feel quite whole again
Incomplete.

Patience

Never thought I would be happy again
Never thought the rain would ever end
Putting this umbrella away for good. It's time to get wet.

Always knew He would come true.
The only One who stayed tried and true.
Cause with Him I'm neva skurred.

You can beat me down once, but never twice
You can chase me for spite, like the 3 blind mice
But you'll never steal my joy.

I can cry and pout, and ask God why
But mine's is not to question
It will come in due time

Trials and tribulations make way for greatness
Evildoers live to prey on my weakness
But my faith never fails me

You can laugh in my face
Look me dead in my eye and smell the fear
Yet neva a scratch be on me when you leave
Live and learn, learn to live
Learning to love Me, plus Myself and I
I was healed.

Confidence and S. Esteem were back in town
And this time for good
I was glowing once again in His glory.

Let your aura shine as bright as the sun
Let everyone see you're a follower of the Son
And neva let them see you sweat.

Neva let them see you defeated.

Neva let them see you give up.

Because HE will neva let you fall.

Reflections: Loving Yourself

Can you complete the mirror activity the main character completed? Can you look in the mirror and say "I love you" and mean it? Try it and write down how it made you feel. Confident, guilty, sad, happy?

_____
_____
_____
_____
_____

Reflections: Playing the Single Game

What is your definition of being 'single and serving God', waiting for him to fulfill your desire for a good, Christian partner to come your way?

_____
_____
_____
_____
_____

Reflections: Defining Your Happily Ever After

Name one way in which you can ensure your own happy ending in life. (No matter what circumstances you may be in.)

_____
_____
_____
_____
_____

Visit the BannermanBooks.com blog to share your *Reflections* from the book.

"Your crown has been bought and paid for. Put it on your head and wear it." ~ Dr. Maya Angelou

About the Author

Cheryl Denise Bannerman, is a multi-genre author of six self-published books and winner of the 2018 Book Excellence Award for her book of poetry, Words Never Spoken.

Within the author's first three works of fiction, Black Child to Black Woman, Words Never Spoken, and A Killer's Reflection, the author addresses critical topics of social concern, such as alcohol and drug addictions, racism and bigotry, domestic abuse and violence, suicide, and child molestation.

In her latest releases, a cozy mystery series entitled the Anna Romano Mystery Series, she hopes to provide relief from a somewhat somber world and spread laughter and smiles with the main character's witty humor and 'unintentional stumbling' over dead bodies and into murder investigations.

Her goal in life is to keep writing and continue helping victims of Domestic Abuse/Violence, Grief and ANON family groups, and Corporate Health and Wellness groups, to heal through words -- encouraging them to 'write the pain' via journaling, and expressing themselves through short stories, songs, and poetry.

She currently resides in Orlando, Florida, where she runs her 25-year-old Training and Development company, specializing in Instructional Design and eLearning.

In her spare time, she loves to read murder mysteries, attend museums, watch movies, try new cuisines, shop with her daughter, and take in the sun on the beach. And, although this author's works are fiction, she has incorporated many of her personal life's experiences into their stories.

What Did You Think of Words Never Spoken?

First, thank you for purchasing this book, **Words Never Spoken**. I know you could have picked any number of books to read, but you picked this book, and for that, I am extremely grateful.

I hope that it added value and quality to your everyday life, and helped you begin the healing process. If so, it would be awesome if you could share this book with your friends and family by posting to social media.

If you enjoyed this book and found some benefit in reading this, I would like to hear from you and hope that you could take some time to post a review online. Your feedback and support will help me to greatly improve my writing craft for future projects and make this book even better.

Visit the web site at www.bannermanbooks.com for contact information.

I want you, the reader, to know that your opinion is very important to me and hope that you will check out my other works of fiction:

Title	*Category/Genre*
Cats, Cannolis, and a Curious Kidnapping	Book 1 of the Anna Romano Mystery Series
A Bloody Stiletto, Cold Lasagna, and a Bestseller	Book 2 of the Anna Romano Mystery Series
Family Ties, Missing Organs, & Champagne	Book 3 of the Anna Romano Mystery Series
A Killer's Reflection	Erotic Psychological Thriller/Serial Killer
Black Child to Black Woman	Women's Fiction/Urban Fiction/Life Stories

www.ingramcontent.com/pod-product-compliance
Lightning Source LLC
Chambersburg PA
CBHW051456290426
44109CB00016B/1784